LiBEARy Skills

(Grade Four through Grade Six)

By
The School Librarians of
Chambersburg, Pennsylvania

Cynthia Drawbaugh
Delores Boggs
Joan Bowen
Susanne Detrich
Darlene Miley
Elizabeth Renshaw
Jean Rieck
Sharon Scheffler
Patricia Sweeney

Cover and inside page illustrations by
Jennifer Ellis

Publishers
T.S. Denison & Company, Inc.
Minneapolis, MN 55431

Standard Book Number: 513-02044-6
LiBEARy Skills – Grade Four through Grade Six
Copyright © 1990 by the T.S. Denison & Co., Inc.
Minneapolis, Minnesota 55431

Table of Contents

Introduction

An Exceptional New Resource that Will Simplify and Clarify Library Use for Your Students.

LiBEARy, the library bears, learn library skills as they become independent investigators in the 4-6 grade level library instruction book. The library planned course of study encourages students to use the library for reference projects and to write reports. The task oriented sheets introduce such skills as arrangement of books, specialized reference materials, research skills, Dewey decimal system, bibliographies, and more! The "hands-on" activities can be taught as individual lessons or can be integrated with the specific grade level curriculum! Beautifully illustrated, easy reference, and educationally wonderful!

GRADE FOUR LIBRARY SKILLS

LiBEARy
Presents
The Bear Facts
About the Library

Table of Contents
Grade Four

The Parts of a Book

Title Page

1. Draw a line from the word to its correct definition.

Title	The person who drew the pictures.
Author	The name of the printer who made the book.
Illustrator	The person who wrote the book.
Publisher	The year in which the book was printed.
Place of publication	The name of the book.
Copyright date	The city in which the book was made.

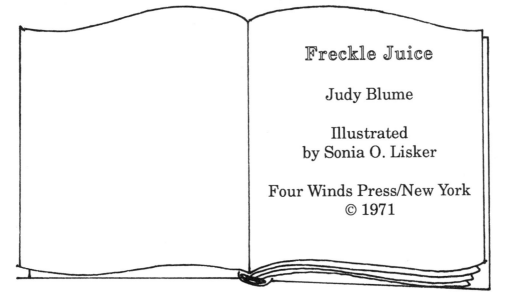

Freckle Juice

Judy Blume

Illustrated
by Sonia O. Lisker

Four Winds Press/New York
© 1971

2. From the title page above, fill in the following information:

Title _____

Author _____

Illustrator _____

Publisher _____

Place of publication _____

Copyright date _____

*Copied from book, *Freckle Juice* by Judy Blume

Table of Contents

By reading the table of contents of a book, you can find the best book for a particular subject or topic. Look at the table of contents given below. Check to see if the topics given in COLUMN II would be found in the table of contents given in COLUMN I. Write the correct chapter numbers in the blanks in Column II.

COLUMN I	COLUMN II
1. The Age of Reptiles	____ A. Horned lizards
2. Are They Poisonous or Harmless?	____ B. Small snakes
3. What Do They Eat?	____ C. What part of the reptile's body is poison?
4. How Do They Move?	____ D. What is an amphibian?
5. Turtles	____ E. When did the age of reptiles begin?
6. Lizards	____ F. How do lizards protect themselves?
7. Snakes	____ G. What do reptiles eat?
8. Amphibians	____ H. Box turtle
	____ I. What color is a garter snake?
	____ J. What is the largest turtle?

Contents
1. The Bear
2. A Bear Story

Glossary

The glossary is found in the back of the book. It gives the definition of the special terms used in that book. It can also be called a "mini-dictionary."

Below is a sample glossary. Use the glossary to answer the questions at the bottom of the page.

* scampering (skam'per ing) running quickly

scold (skold) to point out faults angrily

scoop (skup) to pick up in the hands quickly

scorch (skorch) to burn slightly

scrape (skrap) to rub clean and smooth with a sharp instrument

sear (sir) to burn

shabby (shab'e) wearing old clothes

shawl (shol) cloth worn as a covering for the neck and shoulders

1. Would someone give you shabby clothes as a birthday present? Y or N _____

2. Can a squirrel go scampering through the woods? Y or N_____

3. How many syllables are in the word SCAMPERING?_____

4. Do shawls keep ladies' feet warm? Y or N_____

5. Does the o in SCOLD have a long or short vowel sound?_____

6. Which two words have almost the same meaning_____and_____

7. Do you hear the e in SCRAPE? Y or N_____

8. Could you scoop up an elephant? Y or N_____

*Taken from **Dream and Dragons**, Harper & Row, N. Y., 1980, p. 412

Index

An index is an alphabetical list of the topics in a book or a set of books. It is found in the back of the book. The index tells the pages on which information about each topic will be found.

Main heads listed in the index often have subheads to guide you to other information.

On the right below is a list of questions to look up. Find the important word in each question and look for that word in the index to find the correct page number.

Place the page number on the space provided.

INDEX*

QUESTIONS

____ 1. How do you dance the Hawaiian hula?

____ 2. What are some different ways to say 'hello'?

____ 3. Why do cowboys wear hats?

____ 4. Who wears grass skirts in Hawaii?

____ 5. How are wooden shoes made in Holland?

____ 6. In which country do people wear bamboo hats?

____ 7. How do people in Holland celebrate Easter?

____ 8. Who uses bread hats?

*Taken in abbreviated version from *Childcraft, Holidays and Customs*, Vol. 20
Field Enterprises Educational Corp., Chicago, 1973

Parts of the Book Review

Place the number of the word in front of the correct definition.

1. Cover

2. Spine

3. Author

4. Title

5. Body or text

6. Illustrator

7. Copyright date

8. Publisher

9. Title page

10. Table of contents

11. Glossary

12. Index

_____ A section at the end of a book that gives the meaning of special terms used in the book.

_____ Person who writes the book.

_____ List of chapters or stories in the book.

_____ Company that prints the book.

_____ Person who draws the pictures.

_____ Name of the book.

_____ Page in the front of the book that tells author, title, illustrator and publisher.

_____ Part of the book you see when it is on the shelf.

_____ Date the book was published.

_____ Main part of the book.

_____ Outside part of the book which holds it together and protects the pages.

_____ List of words or topics arranged in alphabetical order, which gives the number of the page on which the information is to be found.

There sure are BEARy many parts to a book.

CARD CATALOG

The card catalog is a guide to help you find books. The cards in the catalog tell you these three things:

1. The titles of all the books in the library.
2. The names of the authors.
3. The names of the subjects in the library, such as ANIMAL STORIES, SPACE TRAVEL, BIRDS and many others.

Some cards found in the card catalog have a band of color at the top. The colored band means the card is not for a book. The colors stand for the following materials:

COLOR	MEDIA	CODING
Blue bands	Filmstrips	Sd/FS
Red bands	Records	Rec
Brown bands	Pictures	Pic
Yellow bands	Cassettes	Cass
Purple bands	Kit	Kit
Green bands	Transparency	Trans
Black bands	Slide	Sl
Bright pink bands	Films (16mm)	Films
Orange bands	Filmloop	FL
Red line under code in call number	Microcomputer disks Microcomputer cassettes Microcomputer cartridges	MC/Disk MC/Cass MC/Cart
Yellow line under code in Call Number	Video Cassettes	VT

Three Types of Catalog Cards

These are examples of the three types of cards you can find in the card catalog for the book **Ramona the Pest** by Beverly Cleary.

Author Card

Cl	Cleary, Beverly
	Ramona the pest; illus by
	Louis Darling. Morrow 1968
	192p illus
	Gr. 3-5

Title Card (Title)

	Ramona the pest
Cl	Cleary, Beverly
	Ramona the pest; illus by
	Louis Darling. Morrow 1968
	192p illus
	Gr. 3-5

Subject Card (Subject)

	SCHOOL STORIES
Cl	Cleary, Beverly
	Ramona the pest; illus by
	Louis Darling. Morrow 1968
	192p illus
	Gr. 3-5

The cards are arranged in alphabetical order in the drawers by the first letter of the top line of the card.

Example: 1. Author card for **Ramona the Pest** would be found in a drawer containing cards beginning with "C" words (Cleary).
2. Title card for **Ramona the Pest** would be found in "R" drawer.
3. SUBJECT card for **Ramona the Pest** would be found in "S" drawer because the subject is SCHOOL STORIES.

A - B	G - H	M	T
C - D	I - K	N - P	U - V
E - F	L	Q - S	W - Z

Cards-Author, Title, Subject

```
┌─────────────────────────────────────────────┐
│                HORSES-STORIES                │
│                                              │
│   He    Henry, Marguerite                    │
│           Justin Morgan had a horse; illus by│
│         Wesley Dennis. Rand McNally   1954   │
│           150p illus                         │
│                                              │
│         Gr. 4-7                              │
│                                              │
└─────────────────────────────────────────────┘
```

Look at the catalog card above and answer the following questions.

1. The author is _____

2. The title is _____

3. The call number is _____

4. Is the book fiction or nonfiction? _____

5. The subject is _____

6. The illustrator is _____

7. The publisher is _____

8. The copyright date is _____

9. The book has _____ pages.

10. Does the book have pictures? Y or N _____

11. The grade level of this book is_____

Card Catalog Drawers

To use the card catalog you must know your alphabet, because all the cards are arranged in alphabetical order.

On the outside of each drawer in the catalog are the letters found in the drawer. These are the GUIDE LETTERS. A card catalog looks similar to this:

1 A - C	3 G - H	5 N - P
2 D - F	4 I - M	6 Q - Z

In the drawer marked "A - C" you will find all the cards beginning with A, B, and C. The other drawers contain the cards for the letters marked on the outside and for all the letters that come between. If you know the title, author or subject of the book you want, the next step is to find the correct drawer.

Author Card

Author cards are put in alphabetical order by the author's last name. If you wanted the book *Ramona the Pest* by Beverly Cleary, look under Cleary, Beverly.

Title Card

Title cards are arranged alphabetically by the first word of the title, unless that word is "A", "An", or "The". Then they are put in order by using the second word. For example, if you were looking for the book called *The Elephant and the Flea*, look under E.

Subject Card

Sometimes you want a book about a particular subject. You can find these books by looking for a subject card. For example, if you wanted a book about snakes, look in the drawer containing the "S" cards for the word SNAKE. Subject cards look different because the subject is typed in capital letters accross the top.

*page 13 has examples of the three types of cards.

Card Catalog Drawers

A	E - F	L	S
B	G	M	T - U
C	H - J	N - Q	V - W
D	K	R	X - Z

In which drawer will you find a card for each of these?

1. ____ A book by Peggy Parish

2. ____ *Charlotte's Web*

3. ____ COOKING

4. ____ A book by Donald Sobol

5. ____ GAMES

6. ____ A book by Margaret Brown

7. ____ *Karting Challenge*

8. ____ *Henry and Ribsy*

9. ____ *Mrs. Piggle-Wiggle*

10. ____ A book by Beverly Cleary

11. ____ *Pinocchio*

12. ____ *Little House on the Prairie*

13. ____ *Album of Horses*

14. ____ DOGS

15. ____ SNAKES

16. ____ FOLKTALES

17. ____ *Pencil, Pen, and Brush*

18. ____ *The Enormous Egg*

19. ____ REPTILES

20. ____ A book by Gene Zion

Name _____ Grade _____

Card Catalog Drawers

THE CARD CATALOG

A - B	I - K	Q - S
C - F	L - M	T - V
G - H	N - P	W - Z

This looks like the front of a card catalog. There are three kinds of cards in the card catalog:

1. Subject Cards
2. Author Cards
3. Title Cards

Which kind of card would you be using to find the following books?
In which drawer would you find the card?

	Kind of Card	Drawer
1. A card for the book, *Reptiles.*	_____	_____
2. Cards that tell you where to find books about HORSES.	_____	_____
3. A card for the book, *Two Is a Team.*	_____	_____
4. Cards that tell you books the library has by Laura Wilder.	_____	_____
5. A card for the book, *The Mouse and the Motorcycle*.	_____	_____
6. Cards that tell you where to find books about DOGS.	_____	_____
7. A card for the book, *Superfudge.*	_____	_____
8. Cards that tell you where to find books about INDIANS OF NORTH AMERICA.	_____	_____
9. Cards that tell you the books the library has by Walter Farley.	_____	_____

Guide Cards

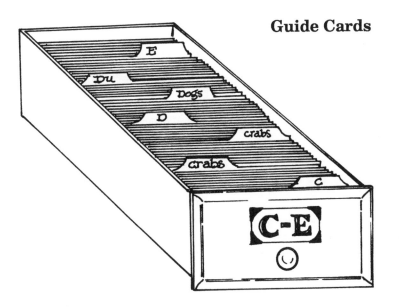

In the catalog drawers are some cards which stand higher than other cards. They have single letters, parts of words, or complete words on them. These are the *Guide Cards.*

Guide cards look like this:

If you wanted a book about DUNE BUGGIES, you would look behind "Du (between "Du" and "E"). If you wanted a book by Beverly Cleary, you would look behind "Ch" (between "Ch" and "Crabs").

Behind which card would you look for the following.

1. DOG-STORIES _____

2. *The Earliest Americans* _____

3. Roger Duvoisin _____

4. *Cabin Faced West* _____

5. William P. DuBois _____

6. EXPERIMENTS _____

7. *Everybody's Weather* _____

8. *Danger Fighters* _____

9. CHEMISTRY _____

10. ENGLAND _____

Name _____ Grade _____

Cards - Author, Title, Subject

```
┌──────────────────────────────────────────────────────────┐
│              HORSES                                        │
│                                                            │
│    636.1     Balch, Glenn                                  │
│    Ba           The book of horses.     Four Winds 1967    │
│                                                            │
│              Gr. 4-6                                       │
└──────────────────────────────────────────────────────────┘
```

1. The author is _____

2. The title is _____

3. The call number is _____

4. Is the book fiction or nonfiction? _____

5. The publisher is _____

6. The copyright date is _____

7. The book is about _____

```
┌──────────────────────────────────────────────────────────┐
│     Ro     Rogers, Mary                                    │
│               Freaky Friday.     Harper & Row 1972         │
│            145p illus                                      │
│                                                            │
│               Gr. 4-6                                      │
│                                                            │
└──────────────────────────────────────────────────────────┘
```

1. The author is _____

2. The title is _____

3. The call number is _____

4. Is the book fiction or nonfiction? _____

5. The publisher is _____

6. The copyright date is _____

Name _____ Grade _____

Card Catalog Search

Find the following subject in the card catalog:

_____

Answer the following questions from the information on the card in the drawer.

1. The author is _____

2. The title is _____

3. The call number is _____

4. Is this book fiction or nonfiction? _____

5. The publisher is _____

6. Does the book have pictures? _____

7. How many pages does this book have? _____

8. The grade level is _____

9. The copyright date is _____

BONUS: Find this book on the shelf.

Ah, my BEARy favorite subject.

ARRANGEMENT OF OUR LIBRARY BOOKS

In order to find books easily and quickly you must learn how the books are put on the shelves. In our libraries you will find two main groups of books, *fiction* and *nonfiction*.

Books of Fiction

A book of fiction is a made-up or imaginary story. Fiction is arranged on the shelves alphabetically according to the first two letters of the author's last name. To make it easier to find the books or to put them on the shelf, the author letters are printed on the spine of the book. The author letters are known as *call numbers*.

This is the way a bookcase of fiction looks:

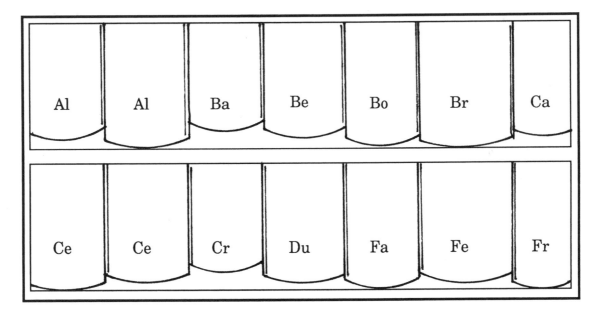

Name _____ Grade _____

Books of Fiction

The call number on a fiction book is made from the first two letters of the author's last name.

What are the call numbers for each of the following books?
Write the call numbers on the line at the the right.

The Lemonade Trick by Scott Corbett   _____

The Real Me by Betty Miles   _____

The Schoolhouse Mystery by Gertrude C. Warner _____

The Black Stallion by Walter Farley   _____

Beezus and Ramona by Beverly Cleary   _____

Sea Star by Marguerite Henry   _____

Lone Hunt by William O. Steele   _____

Homer Price by Robert McCloskey   _____

Old Yeller by Fred Gipson   _____

Across Five Aprils by Irene Hunt   _____

Now using the spaces below, put the call numbers you just completed into proper order as they would appear in the library.

_____ _____ _____ _____ _____

_____ _____ _____ _____ _____

Books of Nonfiction

Most nonfiction books have information about different subjects; but, they can also include books of fairy tales, collections of poetry, and short stories. All of these books are arranged on the shelves by the *Dewey Decimal System of Classification*. It is called Dewey because the idea was thought out by Melvil Dewey. It is called decimal system because a little dot, or decimal (.) is sometimes used, and it is called classification because the books are arranged in classes. Melvil Dewey started this plan of putting books into certain classes, just as you are put into certain classes such as fourth grade, fifth grade, sixth grade, and so on. Books with the same subject have the same number. These call numbers are placed on the spines of the books by the librarian.

A nonfiction bookcase looks like this. Books are arranged by numbers starting with the number that is the lowest and working up to the number that is the highest.

292 Bl	292 De	293 Ma	293.1 Ce	293.1 Fr	293.1 Ma	295 Ba

295 Fa	330 Fr	331 Ad	332 Co	356 Ab	370 Co	372 Sa

Books of Nonfiction

Notice that when there is more than one book with the same number, then the author letters are used to arrange the books alphabetically the same as fiction, like this:

973	973	973	973	973
Ba	Do	Ge	Hi	Mo

The *numbers with the author letters* on nonfiction are also know as *call number*.

Arrange these call numbers on the make-believe books as they are arranged on the shelf in our library. (Be sure to write the number *and* letters.)

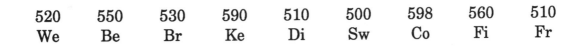

520	550	530	590	510	500	598	560	510
We	Be	Br	Ke	Di	Sw	Co	Fi	Fr

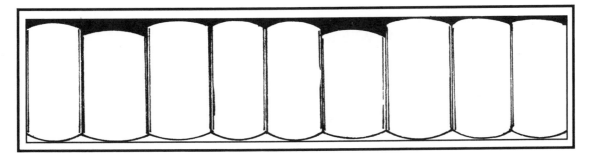

REVIEW
Arrange these nonfiction call numbers in the proper order in the spaces below.

398	596	221	821	973	921	423	636	796	811
Ba	Do	Co	Le	Am	Li	Ea	He	Ra	Ge

_____ _____ _____ _____ _____ _____ _____ _____ _____

Books of Biography

One exception to the rule for making call numbers is biography which is a book about the life of a real person.

1. All such books have the call number 921.
2. Instead of using the author's name, letters for the person written about are used.

EXAMPLE:

Benjamin Franklin　　921
by Charles Graves　　　Fr

ACTIVITY:

Make call numbers for the biographies listed below by writing under the number 921 the first two letters of the last name of the person written about.

1. **Mary Todd Lincoln**　　　　　　921
   by Katherine E. Wilkie　　　_____

2. **Juliette Low**　　　　　　　　921
   by Helen Boyd Higgins　　　　_____

3. **Maria Tallchief**　　　　　　921
   by Elizabeth P. Myers　　　　_____

4. **Davy Crockett**　　　　　　　921
   by Hazel H. Davis　　　　　_____

5. **Amelia Earhart**　　　　　　921
   by Jane Moore Howe　　　　_____

A book about me would be a BEARy biography.

Name _____ Grade _____

REVIEW

1. Arrange these call numbers in the proper order in the spaces provided.

   Ja   Wi   Co   Gr   Re   Sc   Bl   Mi   Wo

   _____   _____   _____   _____   _____   _____   _____   _____   _____

2. Do the call numbers you just arranged belong to fiction or nonfiction books? Circle the correct word - fiction or nonfiction.

3. Arrange these call numbers in the proper order in the spaces provided.

   909   921   973   920   989   921   914   970   940
   Fo   Wa   Ca   Mo   Ro   Li   Ca   Bl   Sh

   _____   _____   _____   _____   _____   _____   _____   _____   _____

4. Do the call numbers you just arranged belong to fiction or nonfiction books? Circle the correct word - fiction or nonfiction.

5. Make call numbers for the biographies listed below. Be sure to include the correct Dewey number and letters.

   _____1. *Daniel Boone, Boy Hunter* by Augusta Stevenson

   _____2. *Abe Lincoln Grows Up* by Carl Sandburg

   _____3. *Paul Revere, Boy of Old Boston* by Augusta Stevenson

   _____4. *Betsy Ross and the Flag* by Jane Mayer

   _____5. *Voyages of Christopher Columbus* by Armstrong Sperry

DEWEY DECIMAL SYSTEM

The numbers for nonfiction books are based on the Dewey Decimal System created by Melvil Dewey. He decided books should be grouped together according to their subject. He made up ten different groups or classes.

These are the ten classes:

000 - Books with many subjects all in one book, such as:
World Book Encyclopedia, Book of Knowledge, Compton's Pictured Encyclopedia, Britannica Junior

100 - Books on how to study and how to think

200 - The Bible, myths

300 - Transportation, government, folklore, holidays, fairy tales

400 - Dictionaries, English and foreign language

500 - Mathematics, astronomy, earth, planets, wild animals, birds, plants

600 - Satellites and space ships, useful arts, how to make things, care of pets, medicine

700 - Drawing, painting, music, games, riddles, sports

800 - Poems, plays, short stories

900 - Books about countries, travel, biography, history

**I can take
a book from
all ten classes
but they are
BEARy heavy.**

Name _____ Grade _____

Dewey Decimal System

The books on this page tell you something about themselves. Write the general Dewey Decimal Classification number on the front of each book. You may use page 28 to do the worksheet.

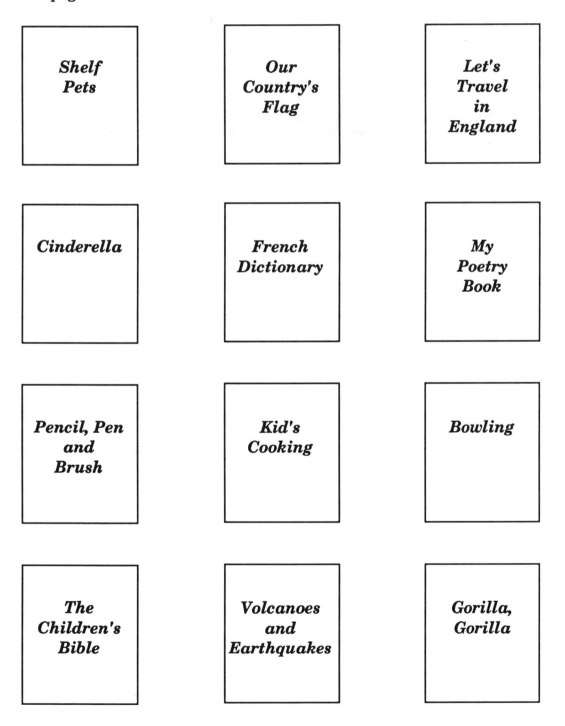

Shelf Pets

Our Country's Flag

Let's Travel in England

Cinderella

French Dictionary

My Poetry Book

Pencil, Pen and Brush

Kid's Cooking

Bowling

The Children's Bible

Volcanoes and Earthquakes

Gorilla, Gorilla

ENCYCLOPEDIAS

How to use Encyclopedias

WHAT IS AN ENCYCLOPEDIA?

A	B	C	D-E	F-G	H	I-J	K-L	M	N-O	P-Q	R-S	T-V	W-Z	INDEX
1	2	3	4	5	6	7	8	9	10	11	12	13	14	15

An encyclopedia is a book or a series of many books that gives important information about people, places, and things. Encyclopedias are valuable sources of information that you will need to use all your lives.

IMPORTANT FACTS ABOUT GENERAL ENCYCLOPEDIAS

1. Encyclopedias are arranged alphabetically like the dictionary or the index of a book. Look at the encyclopedia set above.

2. The set of encyclopedias above has 15 books or volumes.

3. Guide letters are found on the back of each volume to make it easier for you to find information. Sometimes a volume includes only topics beginning with a single letter and other volumes may have several letters. Look at the set above and find the volume which contains four letters of the alphabet within its guide letters.

4. Encyclopedias, like the dictionary, have guide words at the top of each page. Guide words make it easier for you when you look for a topic.

5. Some encyclopedias have an index at the end of each volume or in a separate volume.

How to use Encyclopedias

RULES FOR USING ENCYCLOPEDIAS

1. Look for the last name of a person; for example, Washington, George.

2. Proper names of places or things that are not names of people, look for the first part; for example, New York will be found under *New* York.

3. For a titled person, look under the name and not the title; for example, King John will be found under *John*.

4. For an abbreviation, look for the word as though it were spelled in full; for example, St. Valentine, look for *Saint* Valentine.

REVIEW

A	B	C	D-E	F-G	H	I-J	K-L	M	N-O	P-Q	R-S	T-V	W-Z	INDEX
1	2	3	4	5	6	7	8	9	10	11	12	13	14	15

Using the make-believe encyclopedia above, write in each blank space the number of the volume in which you will find information on each of the following topics:

_____ 1. Amazon

_____ 2. Snakes

_____ 3. Stephen Foster

_____ 4. Magnets

_____ 5. Abraham Lincoln

_____ 6. France

_____ 7. King Henry

_____ 8. Dogs

_____ 9. United States

_____ 10. Mt. Washington

_____ 11. Benjamin Franklin

_____ 12. Pacific Ocean

How to use Encyclopedias

In order to find the answers to the following questions from an encyclopedia, circle the word (or key word) that might be used to find the answer. Then, using page 30, put the number of the volume in which you would find it.

_____ 1. What does the camel carry in its hump?

_____ 2. In what year did Alaska become a state?

_____ 3. How long do whales usually live?

_____ 4. Where was the earliest known library?

_____ 5. How do birds keep cool?

_____ 6. What is the highest waterfall in the world?

_____ 7. What makes a volcano explode?

_____ 8. What is horsepower?

_____ 9. When did baseball first begin in the United States?

_____ 10. In what year was Benjamin Franklin born?

I want to know where the first panda bear in the United States lived.

Name _____ Grade _____

Use an encyclopedia to find some information about:

_____

In the space below, write five (5) important facts about your subject that you could tell to someone.

SOURCE:

_____   _____
Title of Article   Encyclopedia

_____   _____
Volume   Page

Name _____ Grade _____

In the spaces below, copy a question given to you by the librarian. You need to find the answer to this question by using the correct volume of encyclopedia.

Question: _____

_____

_____

Source: _____   _____
          Title of Article   Encyclopedia

_____   _____
          Volume   Page

Answer:

MY **BEARY** FAVORITE BOOKS

1. Call Number _____

   Author _____

   Title _____

2. Call Number _____

   Author _____

   Title _____

3. Call Number _____

   Author _____

   Title _____

4. Call Number _____

   Author _____

   Title _____

5. Call Number _____

   Author _____

   Title _____

6. Call Number _____

   Author _____

   Title _____

GRADE FIVE
LIBRARY
SKILLS

LiBEARy
Presents
BEARy Important Things
About the Library

Table of Contents
Grade 5

SAM AT THE LIBRARY

My librarian
Said to me,
"This is the best book for grade three."
That was the year I was in third,
So I took the book
On her good word.
I hurried home, crawled into bed,
Pulled up the covers over my head,
And turned my flashlight on
And read.

But the book was awful
And icky and bad.
It wasn't funny;
It wasn't sad.
It wasn't scary or terribly tragic,
And it didn't have even an ounce of magic!
No prince,
No dragon,
No talking cat;
Not even a witch in a pointy hat.
Well!
What can you do with a book like that?

My librarian
Tried once more:
"This is the best book for grade four."
That was the year I was in fourth,
So I took her word
For what it was worth;
And I took the book back home to bed,
Draped the covers over my head
Turned my flashlight on,
And read.

But the book was dull as a Brussels sprout.
I couldn't care how the story came out.
It didn't have baseball
Or football or tennis,
It didn't have danger and lurking menace,
Or wicked kings like the ones in history,
And it didn't have even an ounce of mystery!
No midnight moan,
No deserted shack,
No great detective hot on the track,
Nobody tortured on the rack.
So naturally
I took it back.

My librarian
Used her head.
When I was in grade five, she said,
"Sam, it's silly to try to pretend
You like the books I recommend,
When it's perfectly,
Patently,
Plain to see -
Your taste and mine will never agree.
You like sports books -
I can't stand them.
I don't like mysteries -
You demand them.
You think fairy tales are for babies.
You hate dog stories worse than rabies.
You're as different as pickles and stew.
So from now on, Sam,
You go to the shelf,
And pick out the books you want,
Yourself."

And ever since then
We get along fine.
She reads her books;
I read mine.
And if we choose to converse together,
We smile -
And talk about the weather.

By Carol Combs Hole

BOOK WORDS

The book I selected today is

_____
Title

by _____
Author

The call number is

_____

The spine of the book
looks like this.

ARRANGEMENT OF FICTION BOOKS

Fiction books are imaginary stories that were created in the author's mind. The call numbers for fiction books are made up of the first two letters of the author's last name. An example would be **The Westing Game** by Ellen *Ra*skin: Ra.

Circle the call numbers for these fiction books.

1. **It's Like This Cat** by Emily Neville

2. **Ginger Pye** by Eleanor Estes

3. **Rifles for Watie** by Harold Keith

4. **Up a Road Slowly** by Irene Hunt

5. **The Witch of Blackbird Pond** by Elizabeth George Speare

6. **Onion John** by Joseph Krumgold

Put the call numbers in alphabetical order.

1. _____

2. _____

3. _____

4. _____

5. _____

6. _____

ARRANGEMENT OF NONFICTION BOOKS

Nonfiction books contain information, stories that have been handed down from generation to generation, short stories and poetry. Call numbers for nonfiction books are made up of an appropriate Dewey Decimal number and the first two letters of the author's last name. An example would be *The Foxes* by Mark E. Ahlstrom: 599
Ah

1. Nonfiction call numbers are put in order by the number. Try to put these call numbers in order.

| 552 | 523 | 501 | 598 | 568 | 549 | 582 |
| Zi | St | Ma | St | Ti | Ba | Ud |

_____ _____ _____ _____ _____ _____ _____

2. If the numbers are alike, look at the letters to decide which call number would come first. Try to put these call numbers in order.

| 599 | 599 | 599 | 599 | 599 | 599 | 599 |
| St | Ga | Ba | Ma | Sa | Fa | Mi |

_____ _____ _____ _____ _____ _____ _____

Sometimes the call number includes a decimal point and more numbers. In this case, you need to look at the position of the number following the decimal point. For example the call number 599.8 is different from 599.08

St   St

If you were putting these call numbers in order 599.08 would come before

St

599.8.

St

Try putting these call numbers in order.

598.19	598.98	598.09	598.91	598.89
Ke	Jo	De	Ba	Gr

_____   _____   _____   _____   _____

Brain Teasers: Try to put these in order.

591.23	591.3	591.01	591.101	591.035
St	Ba	Gr	Ma	Ni

_____   _____   _____   _____   _____

DEWEY DECIMAL CLASSIFICATION SYSTEM

Why do we have libraries? One person cannot afford to buy all the books he would like to read, therefore libraries make many books available to all of us. Books make our lives richer and happier. We can have friends in books as well as real live friends. If we learn to know our public library and our school library well, the books we find there can entertain us in our free time and help us with our school work.

In most school and public libraries, nonfiction books (books that are not long imaginary stories) are arranged on the shelves by what is known as the Dewey Decimal System of Classification. It is called decimal system because a little dot or decimal point (.) is sometimes used, and it is called classification because the books are arranged in classes. Melvil Dewey started this plan of putting books into certain classes, just as you are put into certain classes such as fourth grade and fifth grade.

Some of the Dewey Classes are as follows:

000	Reference	Encyclopedias
100	Philosophy	Books about the mind and character; how you think and feel
200	Religion	Bible, prayers, and myths
300	Social Science	Government, transportation, education, holidays, legends, folk tales and fairy tales
400	Language	Dictionaries, grammar, and foreign language
500	Science	Books about plants, wild animals, the planets, land forms, weather, dinosaurs and arithmetic
600	Useful Arts	Books on making or doing useful things such as cooking, nursing, homemaking. Also pets, inventions, safety and health, space exploration.
700	Fine Arts	Books on painting, music, dancing, hobbies, crafts, riddles and sports.
800	Literature	Poetry, plays, and short stories
900	History	Books on other countries, biographies and history

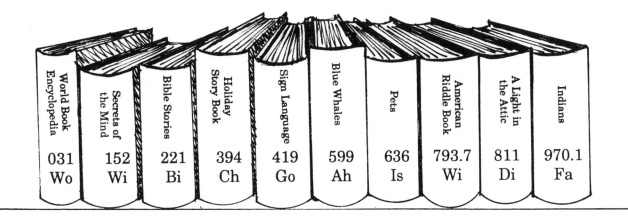

Dewey Decimal Exercise Sheet

The 10 Dewey Categories

All nonfiction books are arranged in number order on the shelves in their Dewey category. On the lines below write the Dewey numbers of the categories in which you would find these books. Here are the 10 Dewey categories. You may also use page 47 to help you.

000-999   General Reference
100-199   Philosophy
200-299   Religion
300-399   Social Science
400-499   Languages
500-599   Science
600-699   Useful Arts and Science
700-799   Fine arts (Art, Music, Sports, Hobbies)
800-899   Literature (Poetry, Plays, Short Stories)
900-999   History, Travel, Biography

Dewey Number

Example: *Exploring the Sun*   500-_____

Familiar Insects of America   _____

The Game of Baseball   _____

Nancy Drew Cookbook   _____

Spanish for Beginners   _____

Let's Travel to France   _____

Johnny Appleseed and Other Poems   _____

World War II   _____

World Book Encyclopedia   _____

The Funny Song Book   _____

Story of Planets   _____

Name _____ Grade _____

Dewey Decimal Partners

Directions: You and another person will be assigned to a shelf of nonfiction. As one person reads the call numbers in order, the other records them. Have the librarian check the call numbers to see if there are any errors present.

_____   _____

_____   _____

_____   _____

_____   _____

_____   _____

_____   _____

_____   _____

_____   _____

_____   _____

_____   _____

_____   _____

_____   _____

Name _____ Grade _____

Dewey Decimal Wheel

Directions: Find a book on the shelf that would fit into each spoke of the Dewey Decimal Wheel. Write down the title and author.

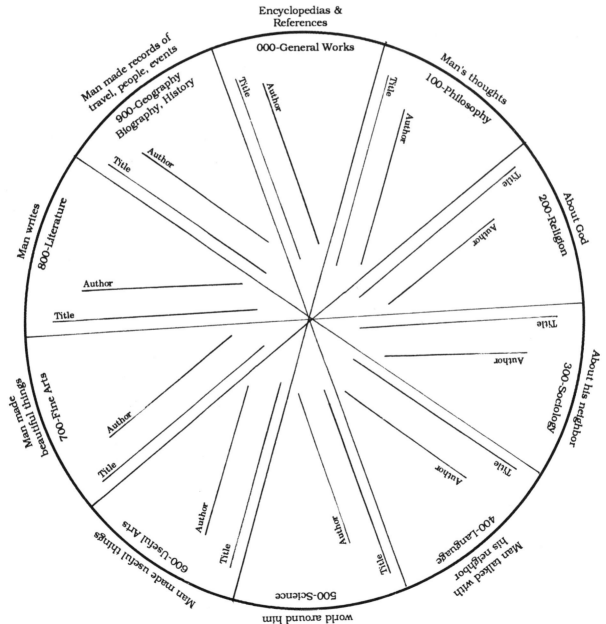

Name _____ Grade _____

Biography

A biography is a book about a real person. All biographies have the call number 921 so they are kept together on the shelves. Since there are so many biographies with this number the letters are created a different way. They are made from the first two letters of the last name of the person the book was about.

If you are looking for a book about Benjamin Franklin you would look for 921 Fr.

Find a biography about someone in whom you are interested.
Answer the questions using your book.

The book is about _____

The title is _____

The author is _____

The call number is _____

The publisher is _____

The copyright date is _____

Write one thing that makes this person famous.

_____

_____

_____

_____

_____

HOW THE CARD CATALOG IS ARRANGED

1. Cards are arranged in alphabetical order by the first word on the top line of the card unless the first word is A, An, or The. Then the cards are arranged by the second word.

2. If a word is abbreviated, it is filed as if it were spelled out.

3. Names beginning with Mc are filed as if they were spelled Mac.

4. Titles with a number in them are arranges as if the number was spelled out.

```
599.09      Johnson, Sylvia
              Animals of the grasslands. Illus. by
            Alcuin C. Dornisch. Lerner Publications Co.
            1976
              28p illus.
              Gr. 4-6

              1. Animals
```

This is a sample catalog card. Examine the card and answer the questions.

1. What type of card is it? _____

2. What is the author's name? _____

3. What is the title? _____

4. What is the publisher's name? _____

5. What is the copyright date? _____

6. How many pages are in the book? _____

7. Does the book have pictures? _____

8. What is the call number? _____

9. Is the book fiction or nonfiction? _____

10. What is the grade level? _____

Name _____ Grade _____

Author Search

When you are looking for a certain author in the card catalog, always look for the author's last name.

Find a book by _____ in the card catalog. Write the:

call number _____

author _____

title _____

grade level _____

```
_____        _____
  Call number              Author

                         _____
                           Title

                         _____
                           Illustrator

                         _____
                           Publisher

  _____
  Copyright date

  _____
     Pages

  _____
   Grade level
```

Locate this book on the shelf and place the paper in the book and put both at the assigned place.

Name _____ Grade _____

Subject Search

When you're looking for the subject of a book always look for the first word if there is more than on word. The subject is what you want your book to be about.

Find a book about _____ in the card catalog. Write the:

call number _____

author _____

title _____

grade level _____

```
┌─────────────────────────────────────────────────┐
│                                                   │
│        SUBJECT _____          │
│                                                   │
│  _____        _____   │
│  Call Number              Author                  │
│                                                   │
│                     _____   │
│                           Title                   │
│                                                   │
│                     _____   │
│                         Illustrator               │
│                                                   │
│                     _____   │
│                          Publisher                │
│                                                   │
│                     _____       │
│                        Copyright date             │
│                                                   │
│                     _____       │
│                           Pages                   │
│                                                   │
│                     _____       │
│                        Grade level                │
│                                                   │
└─────────────────────────────────────────────────┘
```

Locate this book and place this paper in the book and put both at the assigned place.

Name _____ Grade _____

Make Your Own Cards

On your table you will find several books. Choose one. Make an author card. Have your librarian check it. When it is correct make a subject card and title card. Cut out the cards and alphabetize your three cards. Then interfile your cards with the students at your table.

_____   _____
Call number   Author

                             _____
                                         Title

                             _____
                                       Illustrator

                             _____
                                       Publisher

                             _____
                             Copyright date

                             _____
                                       Pages

                             _____
                             Grade level

_____   _____

Call number   Author

_____

Title

_____

Illustrator

_____

Publisher

_____

Copyright date

_____

Pages

_____

Grade level

_____   _____

Call number   Author

_____

Title

_____

Illustrator

_____

Publisher

_____

Copyright date

_____

Pages

_____

Grade level

NEWBERY MEDAL AWARD BOOKS

The Newbery medal is given every year to the author who has made the most distinguished contribution to American children's literature for the preceding year. The award was established by Frederick Melcher in 1921. He named it for John Newbery, an English publisher and seller of children's books.

On the next four pages you will find listed all the Newbery Award Books since 1922. We do not have all these books in our library. Your librarian will assign several titles for you to look up in the card catalog. Put a check in front of the title of each book you find in the card catalog. Place your papers in the assigned place.

Name _____ Grade _____

NEWBERY MEDAL AWARD BOOKS

Year	Title	Author	Call Number
1922	*Story of Mankind*	Hendrik W. Van Loon	(909 Va)
1923	*Voyages of Dr. Doolittle*	Hugh Lofting	(Lo)
1924	*Dark Frigate*	Charles B Hawes	(Ha)
1925	*Tales From Silver Lands*	Charles Finger	(398.2 Fi)
1926	*Shen of the Sea*	Arthur Chrisman	(808.8 Ch)
1927	*Smoky, the Cowhorse*	Will James	(Ja)
1928	*Gay-Neck*	Dhan Mukerji	(Mu)
1929	*Trumpeter of Krakow*	Eric Kelly	(Ke)
1930	*Hitty*	Rachel Field	(Fi)
1931	*Cat Who Went to Heaven*	Elizabeth Coatsworth	(Co)
1932	*Waterless Mountain*	Laura Armer	(Ar)
1933	*Young Fu of Upper Yangtze*	Elizabeth Lewis	(Le)
1934	*Invincible Louisa*	Cornelia Meigs	(921 Al)
1935	*Dobry*	Monica Shannon	(Sh)
1936	*Caddie Woodlawn*	Carol Brink	(Br)
1937	*Roller Skates*	Ruth Sawyer	(Sa)
1938	*White Stag*	Kate Seredy	(Se)
1939	*Thimble Summer*	Elizabeth Enright	(En)

Name _____ Grade_____

NEWBERY MEDAL AWARD BOOKS

Year	Title	Author	Call Number
1940	*Daniel Boone*	James Daugherty	(921 Bo)
1941	*Call It Courage*	Armstrong Sperry	(Sp)
1942	*Matchlock Gun*	Walter Edmonds	(Ed)
1943	*Adam of the Road*	Elizabeth Gray	(Gr)
1944	*Johnny Tremain*	Esther Forbes	(Fo)
1945	*Rabbit Hill*	Robert Lawson	(La)
1946	*Strawberry Girl*	Lois Lenski	(Le)
1947	*Miss Hickory*	Carolyn Bailey	(Ba)
1948	*Twenty-One Balloons*	William Du Bois	(DuB)
1949	*King of the Wind*	Marguerite Henry	(He)
1950	*Door in the Wall*	Marguerite deAngeli	(deA)
1951	*Amos Fortune, Free Man*	Elizabeth Yates	(921 Fo)
1952	*Ginger Pye*	Eleanor Estes	(Es)
1953	*Secret of the Andes*	Ann Nolan Clark	(Cl)
1954	*. . . And Now Miguel*	Joseph Krumgold	(Kr)
1955	*Wheel on the School*	Meindert DeJong	(DeJ)
1956	*Carry On, Mr. Bowditch*	Jean Latham	(921 Bo)
1957	*Miracles On Maple Hill*	Virginia Sorenson	(So)

Name _____ Grade _____

NEWBERY MEDAL AWARD BOOKS

Year	Title	Author	Call Number
1958	*Rifles For Watie*	Harold Keith	(Ke)
1959	*Witch of Blackbird Pond*	Elizabeth Speare	(Sp)
1960	*Onion John*	Joseph Krumgold	(Kr)
1961	*Island of the Blue Dolphins*	Scott O'Dell	(O'De)
1962	*Bronze Bow*	Elizabeth Speare	(Sp)
1963	*Wrinkle In Time*	Madeleine L'Engle	(L'En)
1964	*It's Like This, Cat*	Emily Neville	(Ne)
1965	*Shadow of a Bull*	Maia Wojciechowska	(Wo)
1966	*I, Juan De Pareja*	Elizabeth De Trevino	(Tr)
1967	*Up a Road Slowly*	Irene Hunt	(Hu)
1968	*From the Mixed-Up Files . . .*	E. L. Konigsburg	(Ko)
1969	*High King*	Lloyd Alexander	(Al)
1970	*Sounder*	William Armstrong	(Ar)
1971	*The Summer of the Swans*	Betsy Byars	(By)
1972	*Mrs. Frisby and the Rats of NIMH*	Robert O'Brien	(O'Br)
1973	*Julie of the Wolves*	Jean George	(Ge)
1974	*Slave Dancer*	Paula Fox	(Fo)

Name _____ Grade _____

NEWBERY MEDAL AWARD BOOKS

Year	Title	Author	Call Number
1974	*Slave Dancer*	Paula Fox	(Fo)
1975	*M. C. Higgins, the Great*	Virginia Hamilton	(Ha)
1976	*Grey King*	Susan Cooper	(Co)
1977	*Roll of Thunder, Hear My Cry*	Mildred Taylor	(Ta)
1978	*Bridge to Terabithia*	Katherine Paterson	(Pa)
1979	*The Westing Game*	Ellen Raskin	(Ra)
1980	*A Gathering of Days*	Joan W. Blos	(Bl)
1981	*Jacob Have I Loved*	Katherine Paterson	(Pa)
1982	*A Visit to William Blakes Inn: Poems for Innocent and ExperiencedTravelers*	Nancy Willard	(811 Wi)
1983	*Dicey's Song*	Cynthia Voigt	(Vo)
1984	*Dear Mr. Henshaw*	Beverly Cleary	(Cl)
1985	*The Hero and the Crown*	Robin McKinley	(McK)
1986	*Sarah, Plain and Tall*	Patricia MacLachlan	(MacL)
1987	*The Whipping Boy*	Sid Fleischman	(Fl)
1988	*Lincoln, a Photobiography*	Russell Freedman	(921 Li)
1989	*Joyful Noise: Poems for Two Voices*	Paul Fleischman	(811 Fl)
1990	*Number the Stars*	Lois Lowry	(Lo)

REFERENCE BOOKS

Encyclopedias

Rules to remember when looking up a topic in the encyclopedia.

1. Look for the last name of a person.

2. For a titled person, look under the name, not the title.

3. In words of two or more parts that are not the names of people, look for the first part.

4. For an abbreviation, look for the word as though it were spelled in full.

Underline the word for which you would look in an encyclopedia. Then using the make-believe encyclopedia, write in each blank space below the guide letter(s) on the volume in which you would find that topic.

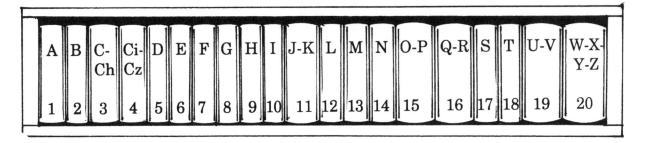

_____1. Queen Isabella

_____2. New York

_____3. San Francisco

_____4. George Washington

_____5. St. Louis

_____6. Mt. Rushmore

_____7. Circulatory system

_____8. Marco Polo

_____9. United States

_____10. Christopher Columbus

Name _____ Grade _____

Encyclopedia Investigation

Choose a person you are studying about in Social Studies class. Find that person in the encyclopedia and answer the following questions:

1. Determine where and when he was born

2. Where he grew up

3. Why he is famous

4. When he died

5. Something about him that you feel is important

I AM STUDYING ABOUT _____

_____

_____

_____

_____

_____

_____

Source of Information:

_____   _____
         Title of Article   Encyclopedia

_____   _____
      Volume   Pages

Name _____ Grade _____

Where in the World Is It?

Select a country or a state from the United States and answer these question. Tell about:

1. An important fact from its history
2. How many square miles this country or state has
3. The population
4. List two chief products
5. Motto
6. Song
7. Places to visit

Don't tell us the name. Let your classmates guess.

_____

_____

_____

_____

_____

_____

_____

_____

Source of Information: _____

Encyclopedia

_____   _____   _____

Title of Article   Volume   Pages

Name _____ Grade _____

Reference Search

Pretend you are making a report on an animal. First choose the specific animal. Then go to the card catalog. Look it up. Find two books in the card catalog. Put the information on the lines provided.

The subject of my report is _____

TITLE _____

CALL NUMBER _____

GRADE LEVEL _____

• •

TITLE _____

CALL NUMBER _____

GRADE LEVEL _____

Find these books on the shelf.

Go to the encyclopedia and look up your subject. Write down the following information.

My subject is _____

I looked in _____ Encyclopedia, Volume _____

The article begins on page _____ and ends on page _____

The article has _____ pages.

The article was written by _____

Children's Magazine Guide

We are able to find information for reports or for our own general knowledge in magazines. A way to speed up finding this information is the use of a magazine index called **Children's Magazine Guide.**

Here is a sample entry from the **Children's Magazine Guide.**
Notice the terms for each item.

Subject	ENDANGERED SPECIES: see also Extinct Animals	Cross-reference
Title	Plight of the Florida Panther. (In-cludes habitat map) J. A. Baggett.	Note Author
Magazine	Sci World Mar 21 '86 p2-4	Page Numbers

Date

DIRECTIONS: Listed below are sample entries from the **Children's Magazine Guide.** Answer the questions related to these entries.

DOGS
   Do You Know These Doggone Dogs?
     M. Bodel. Ranger Rick Mar '87
   p. 37-40+
   Pups Help People with Drug and
     Alcohol Problems.   Cur Sci
   Mar 13 '87 p14

1. The subject of these magazine articles is _____

2. What is the title of the article in the **Ranger Rick** magazine?

_____

3. What is the date of the **Ranger Rick** article? (Month, year) _____

4. Who wrote the **Ranger Rick** article? _____

5. What is the title of the article in **Current Science** magazine?

_____

6. On what page would you find **Pups Help People With Drug and Alcohol Problems**?_____

Children's Magazine Guide: Subject Index to Children's Magazine.
March 1987. Volume 39, Number 7 p. 6

Name _____ Grade _____

Children's Magazine Guide
Exercise Sheet

DIRECTIONS: Choose an entry on any subject from a magazine which we get in the library. Search a column of entries for the name of a magazine you can find useful.

Subject _____

Copy the complete entry.

_____
Title

_____   _____
Author   Magazine

_____   _____
Date   Pages

Locate the magazine in the library. Place your paper in the magazine and put them on top of the card catalog.

REMEMBER: It is possible that the magazine is signed out. So, if you cannot find it after a reasonable search, just turn in your paper.

Atlas

An atlas is a book of maps and related geographical facts. An atlas often contains several kinds of maps for one area. Each map may give information about one feature of the area, such as rainfall, temperature, or natural resources. To locate the place you are looking for you must use the index.

DIRECTIONS: Below is a sample index from *Goode's World Atlas*.
Use the index to answer the questions.

Name	Region	Pronunciation	Page number	Latitude	Longitude
Fairhaven, Ma.	(fâr- hā′vĕn)		111	41.35N	70.55W
Fairhaven, Md.			56d	38.47N	77.05W
Fair Haven, Vt.			111	43.35N	73.15W
Fair I., Scot .	(fâr)		162a	59.34N	1.41W
Fair Lawn, NJ			55	40.56N	74.07W
Fairlee, Md.			56d	38.52N	77.16W
Fairmont, Mn.	(fâr′mŏnt)		115	43.39N	94.26W
Fairmont, WV			111	39.30N	80.10W
Fairmont City, Il.			119e	38.39N	90.05W
Fairmount, In.			110	40.25N	85.45W
Fairmount, Ks.			119 f	39.12N	95.55W
Fairmount Heights, Md.			56d	38.54N	76.55W
Fair Oaks, Ga.	(fâr′ōks)		112c	33.56N	84.33W
Fairport, NY	(fâr port)		111	43.05N	77.30W
Fairport Harbor, Oh.			110	41.45N	81.15W
Fairseat, Eng.			62	51.30N	0.20E
Fairview, NJ			55	40.49N	74.00W
Fairview, Ok.	(fâr′vū)		122	36.16N	98.28W
Fairview, Or.			118c	45.32N	112.26W
Fairview, Ut.			121	39.35N	111.30W

1. In what state would you find Fairmont City? _____

2. On what page would you find Fair Haven? _____

3. What is the latitude for Fairport Harbor _____ N

4. What is the longitude for Fairport Harbor _____W

5. Write the pronunciation for Fairview _____

6. In how many different states could you find a city called Fairview? _____

Goode's World Atlas. Seventeenth ed. Rand McNally. Chicago. 1986 p. 282

National Geographic Index

The *National Geographic Index* helps you quickly locate information from the *National Geographic* magazine. Many times information from these magazine articles can be used when preparing a report for your class. Remember the *National Geographic* magazine contains many articles on states, countries, people, animals, and space.

DIRECTIONS: Below is a sample from the National Geographic Index. Use it to answer the following questions.

BELTSVILLE, MARYLAND:
 • Beltsville Brings Science to the Farm. By Samuel W. Matthews. Contents: Agricultural Research Center. 199-218. Aug. 1953
 •Song of Hope for the Bluebird. By Lawrence Zeleny. Photos by Michael L. Smith. 855-865. June 1977

BELUGAS (White Whales):
 • Three Whales That Flew: By Carleton Ray. Photos by W. Robert Moore. 346-359. Mar. 1962

BENCHLEY, PETER: Author
 • The Bahamas: Boom Times and Bucaneering. Photos by Bruce Dale. 364-395. Sept 1982
 • Bermuda-Balmy. British and Beautiful. Photos by Emory Kristof. 93-121. July 1971
 • Life's Tempo on Nantucket. Photos by James L. Stanfield. 810-839, June 1970
 • New Zealand's Bountiful South Island. Photos by James L. Amos. 93-123. Jan. 1972
 • A Strange Ride in the Deep (on Manta Rays). 200-203. Feb 1981

1. In what state would you find Beltsville? _____

2. Who is the author of *Beltsville Brings Science to the Farm*?

_____

3. In what issue of *National Geographic* would you find *Three Whales That*

  Flew? _____
  month   year

4. What does Peter Benchley do for a living? _____

5. On what pages would you find *Song of Hope for the Bluebird*? _____

6. How many articles did Peter Benchley write? _____

7. What is another name for belugas? _____

National Geographic Index 1947-1983. National Geographic Society. Washington, D. C. 1984 p. 73

Name _____ Grade _____

National Geographic Index
Exercise Sheet

DIRECTIONS: Choose a state. Look up that state in the *National Geographic Index*. Write down the most recent entry. Then try to find the article. Lay this sheet and issue of the magazine on the card catalog.

_____
State

_____
Title

_____
Author

_____
Photos by

_____   _____
Pages   Month , Year

World Almanac

An almanac is published once a year. However, it contains information for previous years. It contains many lists and statistical tables about many different subjects. An almanac is not in alphabetical order. Therefore, you need to use the index to find information.

In the **World Almanac** the index is found in the front. The main entry or main subject is in bold-face type. The sub-entry is a subject related to the main entry and is indented under the main entry. The numbers at the end of each entry stand for the page number.

DIRECTIONS: Below is a sample index from the **World Almanac**. Tell on what page you would find the information to answer the questions.

1. How many potatoes does the United States consume in one year? _____

2. What is the zip code for Harrisburg, Pennsylvania? _____

3. How much did the first postal stamp in the United States cost? _____

4. How many people work for the postal service? _____

5.How many eggs were produced last year in the United States? _____

World Almanac and Book of Facts, 1987. Newspaper Enterprise Association, Inc. New York. 1986 p.23

Name _____ Grade _____

World Almanac
Exercise Sheet

DIRECTIONS: Use the *World Almanac* to answer these questions. Look up the key word in the index which is found in the front of the book. Then look at the indicated page to find your answer. Write down your page number and the answer. The year of my almanac is

_____

1. What is the capital of Connecticut? Page _____ Answer _____

2. When was Arbor Day first observed? Page _____ Answer _____

3. Which team won the World Series of baseball in 1971? Page _____

   Answer _____

4. Who are the two Senators in Congress from Pennsylvania? Page _____

   Answer _____

5. What was the day, month and year that the transcontinental railroad was

   completed? Page _____ Answer _____

6. Who was the inventor of the submarine? Page _____ Answer _____

   _____

7. Make up your own question and find the answer in the *World Almanac*.

   My question is _____

   My answer is _____

Poetry

Many times it is useful to include a poem in a presentation or special program. There are many anthologies or collection of poems. One example is **Time for Poetry** compiled by May Hill Arbuthnot. In this collection you will find a table of contents which lists all the poems with their page numbers. In the back is an index of authors and titles as well as an index of first lines. The table of contents and the two indexes are included to help you quickly find some poems.

DIRECTIONS: Below is a sample index from **Time for Poetry**. Use the author and title index to help you answer the questions.

Daffadowndilly, 191
Daffodils, 191
. . .daffodils, 191
Dance to your daddie, 94
Dandelion, 196
Dandelions, 196
Dark Danny, 14
Davies, Mary Carolyn
        After All and After All, 111; *The Day Before April*, 193; *I'll Wear a Shamrock*, 190
Davies, William Henry
        The Fog, 162; *Leisure*, 203; *The Rain*, 161

1. On what page would you find the poem, "Dark Danny"? _____

2. How many poems by Mary Carolyn Davies are included in this book? _____

3. How many poems are entitled "Daffodils"? _____

4. On what page would you find a poem entitled "The Rain" by William Henry

    Davies? _____

5. On what page would you find "Daffadowndilly"? _____

Arbuthnot, May Hill, comp. *Time For Poetry*, Rev. Ed. Scott. 1961 p. 213.

Name _____ Grade _____

Time for Poetry

DIRECTIONS: Use the table of contents in the front of the book to find a poem

about _____

Copy the title, author and page number of the poem.

_____   _____   _____
          Title   Author   Page

DIRECTIONS: Use the index at the back of the book to find the poem that
begins with the following first line:

_____

_____

On what page is the poem found? _____

Turn to the page and write the title and author of the poem.

_____   _____
                     Title   Author

Authors

Many times it is interesting to know about our favorite authors and illustrators. We can find out about their lives by reading their biographies in *The Junior Book of Authors*, *More Junior Authors*, *The Third Book of Junior Authors* and *The Fourth Book of Junior Authors and Illustrators*. Once we have found the correct volume, the authors and illustrators are arranged in alphabetical order.

DIRECTIONS: Below is a sample index from *The Fourth Book of Junior Authors and Illustrators*. Use the index to answer the following questions.

The following list indicates the volume in which each individual may be found:

J-THE JUNIOR BOOK OF AUTHORS, second edition (1951)

M-MORE JUNIOR AUTHORS (1963)

T-THIRD BOOK OF JUNIOR AUTHORS (1972)

F-FOURTH BOOK OF JUNIOR AUTHORS AND ILLUSTRATORS (1978)

Adams, Adrienne-T	Angelo, Valenti-J	Balch, Glenn-M
Adams, Andy-J	Anglund, Joan Walsh-T	Balderson, Margaret-F
Adams, Julia Davis. *See* Davis, Julia-J	Anno, Mitsumasa-F	Baldwin, James-J
	"Arden, Barbie." *See* Stoutenburg, Adrien-T	Balet, Jan-T
Adams, Katharine-J		"Ball, Zachary" (Kelly Ray Masters)-F
Adamson, Joy-F	Ardizzone, Edward-M	
Adler, Irving ("Robert Irving") -T	Armer, Laura Adams-J	"Bancroft, Laura." *See* Baum, L. Frank-T
	Armstrong, Richard-T	
Adler, Ruth-T	Armstrong, William H.-T	Bannerman, Helen-J

1. In which book would you find an article about James Baldwin?

_____

2. In which book would you find an article about Joan Walsh Anglund?

_____

3. What does the cross reference for Julia Davis Adams tell you to see?

_____

4. In which book would you find an article about Glen Balch?

_____

5. What does the cross reference for Laura Bancroft tell you to see?

_____

DeMontreville, Doris, ed. *Fourth Book of Junior Authors and Illustrators*. Wilson. 1978 p. 361

Name _____ Grade _____

Junior Book of Authors
Third Junior Book of Authors
Fourth Junior Book of Authors
Exercise Sheet

DIRECTIONS: Choose a favorite author. Find an autobiographical sketch of that author by using the index in the **Third Junior Book of Authors** or by looking for the last name at the top of the pages in all books. Write some information about the author.

Author's name _____

Author's dates: Born _____ Died _____

Author's books _____

_____

_____

Interesting facts about the authors's life (at least five).

_____

_____

_____

_____

If you have read one of the authors's books, write a brief book review.

Title of the book _____

Comments _____

_____

Webster's New Biographical Dictionary

Webster's Biographical Dictionary is an alphabetical list of famous people. These people represent various historical periods, nationalities, races, religions, and occupations. Each entry contains information on syllable division and pronunciation.

DIRECTIONS: Below is a sample from **Webster's Biographical Dictionary**. Use it to answer the following questions.

> **Buchanan**, Sir George. 1831-1895. English physician and exponent of sanitary science. Chief agent in eradicating typhus fever, reducing mortality from tuberculosis, and controlling cholera. His eldest son, Sir George Seaton (1869-1936), hygienist, was senior medical officer, Ministry of Health (1919-34).
>
> **Buchanan**, Sir George Cunningham. 1865-1940. British civil engineer, specialist in harbor, dock, and river works.
>
> **Buchanan**, Sir George William. 1854-1924. British diplomatist of Scottish family; ambassador at St. Petersburg (1910-18).
>
> **Buchanan**, James. 1791-1868. Fifteenth president of the United States, b. near Mercersburg, Pa. Grad. Dickinson College (1809). Adm. to bar, Lancaster, Pa. (1812); volunteer in the War of 1812; member, U. S. House of Representatives (1821-31). U. S. minister to Russia (1834-34). U. S. senator (1834-45). Secretary of state (1845-49). U. S. minister to Great Britain (1853-56). President of the United States (1857-61) during years just preceding Civil War; failed to meet challenge of South Carolina's secession (Dec. 20, 1860), and endeavored to avoid the issue of civil conflict.

1. For what is James Buchanan famous? _____

_____

2. From what country is Sir George William Buchanan? _____

3. When did Sir George Cunningham Buchanan die? _____

4. What occupation did Sir George Buchanan have? _____

5. Where was James Buchanan born? _____

Webster's Biographical Dictionary. G. & C. Merriam Company. Srpingfield, Massachusetts. 1976 p. 208

Name _____ Grade _____

Webster's New Biographical Dictionary
Exercise Sheet

Choose a person's name you know very little about.

_____
Name

Give the dates of the person's life.

_____   _____
Birth   Death

Write some information about the person including what the person is know best for doing. Write at least five facts.

_____

_____

_____

_____

_____

_____

_____

Place this paper at the collection place.

Webster's New Geographical Dictionary

Webster's New Geographical Dictionary provides information about places throughout the world. The places are listed in alphabetical order. Each entry contains information about spelling and pronunciation. Some entries also contain information about location, population, size, economy, and history.

DIRECTIONS: Below is a sample from **Webster's New Geographical Dictionary**. Use it to answer the following questions.

> **Cham·bal** \ 'chem-bel\. Unnavigable river, cen. India; rises in W Vindhya Mts. near Indore and flows NE, E, and SE into the Yamuna W of Kanpur.
>
> **Cham·ber·lain** \'cham-ber-,lan\. City   of Brule co., S South Dakota, on Missouri river 10m. N of its confluence with White river; opo. (1980c) 2258; stock raising.
>
> **Chamberlain Lake**. Lake in N Piscataquis co., N cen. Maine
>
> **Chamb·bers** \ 'cham-berz\. 1 Island in Green Bay, NE Wisconsin, in Door co.
> 2 Name of counties in two states of the U.S. See tables at ALABAMA and TEXAS.
>
> **Cham·bers·burg** \ 'cham-berz-,berg\. Industrial borough.   of Franklin co., S Pennsylvania, 50 m. WSW of Harrisburg. pop. (1980c) 16.174; limestone, freestone, marble quarries Wilson Coll. (1869); settles 1730; burned by Confederates 1864.

1. In what state would you find Chamberlain City? _____

2. In what country is Chambal? _____

3. In what state would you find Chambersburg? _____

4. What kind of stone would you find near Chambersburg? _____

5. What river is Chamberlain near? _____

6. When was Chambersburg burned by the Confederates? _____

Webster's New Geographical Dictionary. Merriam-Webster Inc. Springfield, Massachusetts. 1984 p. 240

Name _____ Grade _____

Webster's New Geographical Dictionary
Exercise Sheet

Choose a place in the world that you know very little about.

_____

Name of Country or City

Write the pronunciation.

_____

Write some information about the place. Write at least five facts.

_____

_____

_____

_____

_____

_____

_____

_____

Place this paper at the collection place.

BIBLIOGRAPHY OF FAVORITE BOOKS
I HAVE READ

1. _____   _____   _____
   Call Number   Author   Title

   _____   _____   _____
   Place of Publication   Publisher   Copyright Date

2. _____   _____   _____
   Call Number   Author   Title

   _____   _____   _____
   Place of Publication   Publisher   Copyright Date

3. _____   _____   _____
   Call Number   Author   Title

   _____   _____   _____
   Place of Publication   Publisher   Copyright Date

4. _____   _____   _____
   Call Number   Author   Title

   _____   _____   _____
   Place of Publication   Publisher   Copyright Date

5. _____   _____   _____
   Call Number   Author   Title

   _____   _____   _____
   Place of Publication   Publisher   Copyright Date

GRADE SIX
LIBRARY
SKILLS

LiBEARy
Rolls
Into Learning
With
Books
Magazines and Reference Materials

Table of Contents
Grade Six

Card Catalog Review

FIRE FIGHTERS

628.9   Loeper, John J
Lo   By hook and ladder: the story of fire
        fighting in America. Atheneum 1981
        74p illus bibl

        A history of fire fighting including
        information on firemen, female fire-
        fighters, fire engines, fire fighting
        techniques, and some famous fires in
        American history.
        1. Fire fighting 2. Fire fighters
        I. Title

Look at this sample card from the card catalog and answer the following questions.

1. What is the title of the book?_____

2. Who is the author?_____

3. What is the call number of the book?_____

4. Is the book fiction or nonfiction?_____

5. What type of card is shown in this example?_____

6. Who is the publisher?_____

7. How many pages are in the book?_____

8. What is the copyright date?_____

9. Does this book have pictures?_____

10. What is the subject of the book?_____

Card Catalog

A card in the catalog gives you information about a book. Look for a SUBJECT CARD in the card catalog. Then, on the line below, fill in the information asked for from the card.

_____   _____
Call Number   Subject

_____
Author

_____
Title

_____
Publisher

_____
Copyright Date

Name ———————————————— Grade ——————————

Card Catalog

A card in the catalog gives you information about a book. Look for a TITLE CARD in the card catalog. Then, on the line below, fill in the information asked for from the card.

————————————————
Call Number

————————————————————————
Author

————————————————————————
Title

————————————————————————
Publisher

————————————————————————
Copyright Date

Card Catalog

A card in the catalog gives you information about a book. Look for an AUTHOR CARD in the card catalog. Then, on the lines below, fill in the information asked for from the card

_____
Call Number

_____
Author

_____
Title

_____
Publisher

_____
Copyright Date

Reference Books

Reference books are used when you are working on a research project. Different types of reference books are used to find different types of information.

Encyclopedia - Information on many things–people, places, ideas

Dictionary - Pronunciations and meanings of words

Atlas - Collection of maps

Almanac - Up-to-date facts, charts, tables

Which reference book would you use to find the answers to the following questions?

1. Where and when was Abraham Lincoln born? _____

_____

2. The meaning of the word, kauri. _____

3. A map of Europe. _____

4. The population of New York City. _____

5. The top ten movies of 1989. _____

6. The events leading to the Civil War. _____

7. The pronunciation of the word, phenomenology. _____

8. The location of Humpheys Peak. _____

World Almanac

The **World Almanac** is a specialized reference book. A new edition is published every year with up-to-date facts. There are two indexes in the almanac - Quick Reference Index and a General Index.

Steps in Using the **World Almanac**

1. Define the question
2. Pick out the key words
3. Look up the key words in the index
4. Look on page(s) given in index
5. Skim the page to find the answer

Use the index in the **Almanac** to answer the following questions. Remember to pick out the key words in the questions.

1. What country won a total of 9 medals in the 1984 Winter Olympics?

2. What is the address of the Chicago Bears football team?

3. Which Amendment limits the Presidential term of office?

4. What is the 4th largest volcano in North America? How high is it? Where is it located?

5. What is the zip code and area code of Santa Barbara, California?

6. What were the highest and lowest temperatures ever recorded in Harrisburg, Pennsylvania?

7. What is the original name of Pat Benatar?

Reader's Guide To Periodical Literature

The **Reader's Guide** is a reference tool that indexes periodical articles.

Here is a sample entry from the **Reader's Guide to Periodical Literature**. Study it carefully, then answer each of the questions below.

VEGETABLE GARDENING

    Complete vegetable garden: In your own backyard,
      B. Garrett. il. Bet Hom & Gard 52: 84-7
    Ap '74

---

1. What is the entry heading? ——————————————————

2. What is the title of the article? ——————————————

3. Who is the author of the article? ——————————————

4. Does the article have pictures? ——————————————

5. What is the name of the magazine? ——————————————

6. What is the volume number of the magazine? ————————

7. On what pages of the magazine would you find this article? ————

8. What month of the magazine is needed? ——————————

9. What year is the magazine? ————————————————

Reader's Guide to Periodical Literature

Look up the subject _____
in the **Reader's Guide to Periodical Literature**.

Fill in the following information about one magazine article about your subject

1. Title: _____

2. Author: _____

3. Magazine: _____

4. Page Number(s): _____

5. Month, Day, Year: _____

Reader's Guide to Periodical Literature Review

> Bicycles
>   See also
>   Cycling
> A guide to buying bikes. J. Merline. il. Consum Res Mag
>   68:26-9 0 '85

1. What is the entry heading? _____

2. What is the date of the magazine? _____

3. What is the name of the magazine? _____

4. Does this article have pictures? _____

5. What is the title of the magazine article? _____

6. What is the volume number of the magazine? _____

7. Who wrote the magazine article? _____

8. On what pages can the article be found? _____

Research Projects

The following steps should be followed when doing research projects.

1. Define the question you want to answer.
2. Use various reference materials (card catalog, periodicals, encyclopedias, almanacs, etc.).
3. Take notes and record sources.
4. Ask the librarian for additional help.
5. Organize notes in outline form.
6. Write the report.
7. List the references used in the report - make a bibliography.

Choose a topic for a Research Project

Reference materials (3 different sources) that you will use in doing your research.

1. ——————————————————————————————————

——————————————————————————————————

2. ——————————————————————————————————

——————————————————————————————————

3. ——————————————————————————————————

——————————————————————————————————

Name _____ Grade _____

Take Notes

After selecting the three reference sources, use this page to take notes. Do not copy from the materials, but write the information in your own words. Use key words and write short phrases. Later you can write sentences.

_____

_____

_____

_____

_____

_____

_____

_____

_____

_____

_____

_____

_____

Be sure to record the:

Source _____

Title _____

Article _____

Volume _____

Pages _____ for each reference book you use.

*Note to the teacher
   Specific instruction may be given as to what information is needed when taking notes.

Name _____ Grade _____

Outline

Notes need to be organized in outline form before writing a report. An outline organizes facts into main topics and subtopics. Use this workpage to write an outline.

SAMPLE FORM:

I. (Main topic) _____

    A. (Subtopic) _____

    B. (Subtopic) _____

II. (Main topic) _____

    A. (Subtopic) _____

    B. (Subtopic) _____

Writing a Report

After the notes are taken and the outline is formed, it is time to write the report. Write your "rough draft" for your report on this page.

_____

_____

_____

_____

_____

_____

_____

_____

_____

_____

_____

_____

_____

_____

_____

_____

_____

_____

_____

Bibliography

A bibliography is a selected list of books and other materials on a certain subject. It is important that you include a list of the materials at the end of the report.

Use the following form as a guide in making your bibliography:

BOOK

Author. Title. Place of Publication: Publisher, Date. Pages (if using only part of the book)

Ex.   Madison, Arnold. Drugs and You. New York: Messner, 1971. pp. 16-21

ENCYCLOPEDIAS

Author (if given). "Title of Article," Name of Encyclopedia. Year. Volume, Pages.

Ex.   Piccard, Don. "Balloon," The World Book Encyclopedia. 1964. vol. 2, pp. 39-44

MAGAZINES

Author. "Title of Article," Name of Magazine, Volume, Pages, Date

Ex.   Lewis, C. "Navy Unveils Low-Cost Sounding Rocket," Aviation World, vol. 69, pp. 49-51, November 3, 1968

FILMSTRIPS

Title. Producer, Date.

Ex.   The Old and New in South America. Curriculum Films, 1951.

OTHER AV
(Transparencies, pictures, etc.)

Title. Producer, Type of material.

Ex.   Stars. Eye Gate, transparency.

Name _____ Grade _____

Bibliography

Your bibliography for the report can be written on this page. Use page 99 as a guide to make a bibliography.

1.

2.

3.

4.

Name _____ Grade _____

FINAL REVIEW

I. Write true or false for each statement.

_____   1. The card catalog is a guide to materials found in the library.

_____   2. There are at least 6 types of cards for each book in the library.

_____   3. On an author card, the author's last name is first.

_____   4. When looking for the title card *The Black Stallion*, you should look up the word **The**.

_____   5. On a subject card, the subject is found on the top line typed in capital letters.

_____   6. You can find information about audiovisual materials in the card catalog.

_____   7. There are 10 classes of books in the Dewey Decimal System.

_____   8. A biography is a book about a person's life.

_____   9. An almanac is a book of maps.

_____   10. A copyright gives you the right to copy materials from a book.

II. From the catalog card below, answer the following questions.

HORSES

682   O'Connor, Karen
O'C   Try these on for size, Melody.
Dodd, 1983.
45p. illus

Gr. 6-7

1. Horses 2. Blacksmithing
I. Title

1. The title of the book is _____

2. The author's name is _____

3. The copyright date is _____

4. The call number is _____

5. Who is the publisher? _____

6. How many pages are in the book? _____

7. Is the book fiction or nonfiction? _____

8. What type of card is shown in this example? _____

9. Does this book have pictures? _____

10. What is the subject of the book? _____

III. Using the information from the **Reader's Guide** sample in the box below, answer the following questions.

SPORTS
    See also
    College athletics
    Recreation

    Competitions
    Flying High! C. Rinder. il Seventeen
    40:46 Ap '81

1. What is the name of the magazine? _____

2. What is the entry heading? _____

3. What is the date of the magazine? _____

4. What are the "see also" subjects? _____

5. What is the title of the article? _____

6. What is the volume number of the magazine? _____

7. Who is the author of this magazine? _____

8. What is the subheading of the magazine entry? _____

9. On what page(s) can the article be found? _____

10. What does "il" mean? _____

IV. Select the correct term from the following list and write it on the line provided. Match the term with its meaning.

Almanac   Call number   Fiction
Atlas   Card catalg   Nonfiction
Author   Copyright date   Publisher
Author card   Dewey Decimal Classification   *Reader's Guide*
Bibliography   Dictionary   Subject card
Biography   Encyclopedia-General   Title
                     Encyclopedia-Special   Title card

_____ 1. Contains cards for all materials in the library arranged in alphabetical order

_____ 2. A person who writes a book.

_____ 3. A story of a person's life.

_____ 4. A book or set of books containing knowledge and facts on many subjects.

_____ 5. Books that contain true information.

_____ 6. A catalog card that has the title of the book on the top line.

_____ 7. The company who prints, binds and distributes the material in a book or magazine.

_____ 8. A yearly publication which lists current information.

_____ 9. A book or set of books containing knowledge and facts on a special subject.

_____ 10. A list of books on a special subject.

_____ 11. The system of numbers used to mark and arrange nonfiction books.

_____ 12. A catalog card that has the subject of the book on the top line.

_____ 13. A long imaginary story.

_____ 14. The name of the book.

_____ 15. A catalog card that has the author's name on the top line.

_____ 16. The date the book was published.

_____ 17. A book of maps.

_____ 18. An index to magazine articles.

_____ 19. A book that has an alphabetical list of words with their meanings.

_____ 20. The number and author letters found on the spine of the book and also in the upper left-hand corner of the catalog card.

V. The Dewey Decimal System is a method of classifying books, developed in 1876 by Melvil Dewey. The system classifies books in ten main categories.

000   General Works and Encyclopedias

100   Philosophy

200   Religion

300   Social Sciences

400   Language

500   Natural Science

600   Useful Arts

700   Fine Arts and Recreation

800   Literature

900   History and Biography